HARDPRESS.NET
HOME OF HARD-TO-FIND BOOKS

Religio Laici
by Charles Blout

Address:
HardPress
8345 NW 66TH ST #2561
MIAMI FL 33166-2626
USA
Email: info@hardpress.net

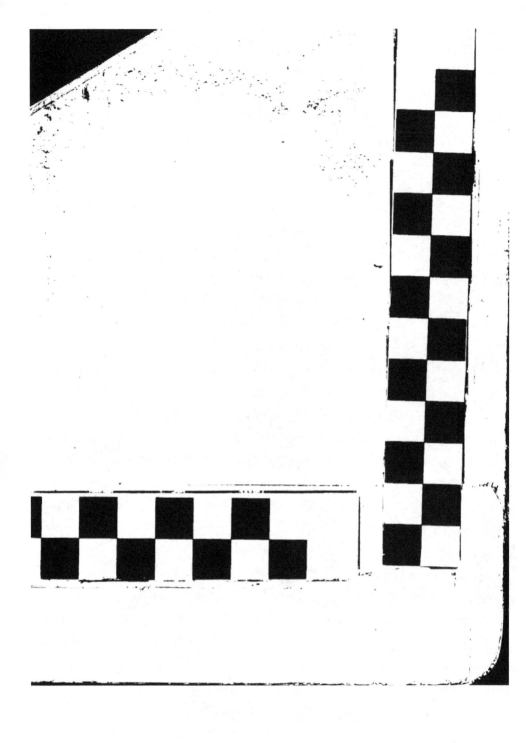

828
D8r
B66
16

Iount, Charles

RELIGIO LAICI.

Written in a Letter to
JOHN DRYDEN Esq.

Juvenal, Sat. 8.

*Quod modo proposui non est
Sententia, verum
Credite me vobis folium
recitare Sibyllæ.*

LONDON,

Printed for *R. Bentley*, and
S. Magnes, in *Russel street*, in
Covent-garden. 1683.

TO HIS
Much Honoured Friend
JOHN DRYDEN Esq.

SIR,

THE Value I have ever had for your Writings, makes me impatient to peruse all Treatises that are crown'd with your Name; whereof, the last that fell into my Hands, was your *Re-*

ligio

ligio Laici ; which expref-
fes as well your great Judgment in, as Value for Religion : a thing too rarely
found in this Age among
Gentlemen of your Parts ;
and, I am confident, (with
the Blessing of God upon
your Endeavours) not un-
likely to prove of great
Advantage to the Publick ;
since, as *Mr. Herbert* well
obferves,

> *A Verse may find him, who*
>   *a Sermon flies,*
> *And turn Delight into a*
>   *Sacrifice.*

We

Dedicatory.

We read in Ancient Times, before the Institution of *Moral Philosophy* by *Socrates*, that *Poets* in general were to the People in stead of their *Sacred Writ*, from whom they received their *Divinity*, and Opinion concerning the *Gods* ; as, who, and how, to be worshipped , how pleased and pacified, by what *Prayers* and *Ceremonies* , together with such *Rites* and *Ceremonies* as were the *Dionysiaca, Cybeliaca, Isiaca, Eleusiniaca,* and

the

the like, Instituted by *Orpheus*. All which were built upon this Ground, That there could be no true *Poet* but must be Divinely inspired; and if Divinely inspired, then certainly to be believed. This we find largely disputed and asserted even by *Philosophers* of best Account in those Days. But the two main Arguments induced them to that Belief, were; *First*, That extraordinary Motion of Mind wherewith all good *Poets*

in

in all Ages have been pof-
feffed and agitated : And,
fecondly, The Teftimony of
Poets themfelves, who pro-
feffing themfelves Infpired,
have made particular Relations of ftrange Vifions,
Raptures, and Apparitions
to that purpofe : So that
as the Beginning, Growth,
and Confirmation of Ido-
latry may be afcribed (as
by many it is) to *Poets*, and
their Authority ; fo alfo to
fuppofed *Enthufiafms* and
Infpirations, upon which
that Authority was chiefly

grounded. Hence it is, that many Ancient Authors, as *Aristotle*, *Strabo*, and others, affirm, That *Poetry* (in matter of *Writing* and *Composition*) was in use long before *Prose*: which might seem strange, if not incredible, did we judge by the Disposition of later Times; but of those *Enthusiastick Times*, not less probable, than certain, as our Learned *Casaubon* well observes. And this I thought fitting to premise, in Answer to that

that Obection which your Modesty is so apprehensive of, *viz.* That being a *Laick*, you interpose in Sacred Matters.

Rapin (in his *Reflexions*) speaking of the necessary Qualities belonging to a *Poet*, tells us, *He must have a Genius extaordinary, great Natural Gifts, a Wit just, fruitful, piercing, solid, and universal ; an Understanding clean and distinct ; an Imagination neat and pleasant ; an Elevation*

of

of Soul, that depends not only on Art or Study, but is purely a Gift of Heaven, which muft be fuftained by a lively Senfe and Vivacity; Judgment, to confider wifely of Things; and Vivacity, for the beautiful Expreffion of them, &c. Now this *Charaƈter* is fo juftly *yours,* as I cannot but think that he defcribed what a great *Poet* fhould be, by hearing what *you* were; and the rather, fince I have been informed by fome *Englifh* of his Acquaintance, That

Mon-

Monsieur Rapin was studious in our Language, only for your sake : Nor would his Pains be lost.

'Tis a Question not easily to be decided , Whether you have been more serviceable to the Peace of the *State* in your *Absolom and Achitophel*, or to the *Church* in your *Religio Laici*, or to the *Nobility* and *Gentry* in the innocent Recreation of your *Plays* ? A Country - Retirement, like that of *Ovid's*, to one

that

that has led the Spring of his Age, and Vigour of his Youth, among the Noise and Pleasures of the Town, is certainly a Transformation no less disagreeable, than that which the *Poets* feign of *Acteon*, or *Sacred Writ* of the *Assyrian Monarch*, who grazed with the *Beasts* of the Field; and to abandon a *Covent-Garden* Society for the Insipid Dull Converse of a Country Village, (where the Nomination of New Healths is the heighth

heighth of their Inventi-
on) would render a *Rural
Life* to be no less than a
Civil Death, were it not
for *Mr. Dryden's* Writings,
which keep us still alive,
and, by a most Natural
Representation of the Hu-
mours of the Town, make
us flatter and fansie our
selves (like the Enjoyment
of a Lover's Dream) to be
still there.

But I shall wave these
Acknowledgments to you,
as things too general to
be

be engroffed by me alone,
And will now fpend the
Remainder of this *Epiftle*
in informing you of the
Occafion of my troubling
you with this fmall *Piece*,
which I Entitle by the
Name of *Religio Laici*,
from a Treatife of the
Lord Herbert of *Cherburie's*
fo called ; whofe *Notions*
I have often made ufe of,
and grounded the Chief
of my Difcourfe upon his
Five Catholick or *Univer-*
fal Principles : Wherein
my only Aim is, to affert
an

an *Universal Doctrine*, such as no ways opposeth the Religion Established: among us, and which may tend both to the Propagation of Vertue, and Extirpation of Vice, as well as to the Reconciliation of those *Dissenters* now in *England*, who have of late so disturbed the Quiet of this Realm, and who, under the Pretence of Religion, would exclude all *Governours* but *themselves*. For, as a late

Author

Author well observes, *Every Opinion makes a Sect; every Sect, a Faction; and every Faction (when it is able) a War: and every such War is the Cause of God; and the Cause of God can never be prosecuted with too much Violence: So that all Sobriety is Lukewarmness; and to be Obedient to Government, Carnal Compliance.* Which are the Opinions of those that would rob *Cæsar* of his Due, as well as re-
move

move the Peoples *ancient Land-marks.*

But for my part, as in *Civil Politicks*, I would not, in this so *Ancient* and so *Lineal* a *Monarchy,* abandon the Beams of so fair a *Sun,* for the dreadful Expectation of a divided Company of *Stars*; so neither, in *Ecclesiasticks,* do I covet to be without the *Pale* of the *Church :* since, though I will not *Dogmatically* affirm, (as some

some do) That *Episcopacy* is *Jure Divino*; yet (with the *Lord Bacon*) I say, and think *ex Animo*, That it is the nearest to *Apostolical Truth*, and the most coherent with *Monarchy*: Wherein, I know, you will not differ from me.

And therefore, *Sir*, at this time, when the *Name* of *Christ* is made use of to palliate so great Villanies and Treasons, un-

der

der the Pretext of *God's Cause*, againſt both *King* and *Government*, I thought I could do no leſs than ſnatch up all *Weapons* that might defend the *Publick*, and hope I have not lighted upon one with a *double Edge.*

I have endeavoured that my Diſcourſe ſhould be onely a Continuance of yours ; and that, as you taught Men how to *Believe*, ſo I might in-
ſtruct

ſtruct them how to *Live.*
For, as Dr. *Donne* well
obſerves, Though *Chriſti-*
anity is the *Fort* or *Citadel,*
yet *Vertue* and *Moral Ho-*
neſty are its *Fences* and
Out-works, whereby alone
it is teneable. Wherefore,
I deſigned this Treatiſe of
mine to be onely an *Ad-*
dition, or rather the *Con-*
ſequence of yours ; encou-
raging Men to Live up
to the *Vertue* of that *Do-*
ctrine you teach. Which
-with your Pardon for the
preſent,

prefent, and Friendfhip for the future, is the higheft *Ambition* of,

S I R,

Your moft Faithful Friend, and Servant,

C. B.

Religio Laici.

The Occasion of this Treatise.

THere is not any Meditation hath given me greater trouble, than when I think, That a Doctrine fo neceffary, as the Knowledge of God, with the true Way to ferve and worfhip him, together with the Means to attain everlafting Salvation, fhould be fo varioufly deliver'd and taught in divers Ages and Countries; as alfo urged in fuch perplext and difficult terms; (which by the many Volumes

B of

of this Argument, in several Languages, may appear;) And after all this, yet to find it presented to me under such terrible Menaces and Execrations, as if, among the many Churches in the World, I did not adhere to the right, (which each claimed to be theirs) I could not justly hope for salvation; but, on the contrary, expect eternal Torture, without any prospect of Relief.

Being therefore in this doubtful and dangerous condition, I did at last conclude with my self, that one of these two things was to be done:

Methods of Enquiry into Religion.

First, That (notwithstanding the Affronts and Threats wherewith

with the Priests on every side
would deter us from all other
Religions, as well as Invitati-
ons, Promises, and comfortable
Doctrines, by which they
would draw us to their own, in
any particular Church,) I was
bound, either to study with an
impartial mind, not only all
the several Religions; but likewise the Controversies amongst
them in divers Ages, Languages and Countries. And for this
purpose, not only to acquire
the Tongues used heretofore,
or at this present time throughout the Universe: But also to
read the several Authors that
have written upon these Arguments; and together with them
to confer those Learned men,
who (though they had not pub-
lished any thing in writing)

might

might yet be no lefs able to edi-
fie me, than the former. Or,

Secondly, To fix upon fome
Fundamental Articles agreed
upon by all that I could meet
with, and confider afterwards
how far they might conduce to
my falvation.

The former of thefe two I
foon perceiv'd to be impoffible;
for, whofe private Affairs at
home, or publick Duty to his
Native Country, will permit
him to take fuch Journies to all
the Quarters of the World?
Whofe Eftate or Revenue will
furnifh him with Money for fo
long and great an Undertaking?
Or whofe Conftitution is of that
ftrength and ability, that, were
he to efcape all the Dangers he
muft inevitably meet with,
could yet undergo fo immenfe a
travel

travel and labour? Whofe Memory could either contain all
the Works of the feveral Languages and Religions; or Judgment decide the different Opinions and Faiths pretended under the Authority of fo many
great Churches? which courfe
yet unlefs he purfued to the
end, he could not with Juftice fay he had performed his
Duty. For fince the determin-
ing finally of any matter of Importance, where Parties are not
heard on all fides, is not only
againft common Reafon, but
contrary even to the ordinary
practice of Juftice in all other
cafes; he muft think himfelf in
that the moft important and fe-
rious bufinefs that can befall
Mankind, obliged to make as
particular and exact a fearch

and examination of Religions,
as is possible.

But here we will suppose,
that after diligent Enquiry, one
might learn what was taught in
this or that Country, under
some general Notions; (though
no where sufficiently, according
to all the Tenents, Rites, and
Ceremonies taught or practised
amongst them,) yet how could
the knowledge of any one Religion alone give him satisfaction, especially when he should
find it controverted in some
other Country, and where as
able men, at least in all other
points of Learning, might in
great numbers be found? Shall
he, because his Birth or Affecti-
on enclines him to one Country
or Religion more than another,
so factiously embrace it, as to
think

think no other to be good or
acceptable to God, where men
do the best they can to serve
him, and live well? Must he
prejudge all other Religions as
erroneous and false, when as
yet he hath not heard what
they can alledge for the justi-
fying of their Faith? No; but
too too many are guilty of this
Partiality; for that, *till we receive a Spirit of Judgment to
discern the right way, every way
is thought to be wrong, but that
which we are brought up in:
And pious Education doth the
same in this latter Age, which
Miracles did formerly;* as the
Learned *Gregory* well observes.

Howbeit, because something
here must be attempted, lest
we should seem wholly to for-
sake our selves, I did in my particular

ticular conceive nothing so proper for my purpose, as to look
upon those Countries chiefly
from whence all other Learning
and Sciences did originally flow;
which   consideration,   as it
brought me to those Provinces
wherein the *Greek Tongue* did
anciently flourish, as contain-
ing in it self alone almost all
humane Literature : So, when I
found the Inhabitants thereof
in so miserable an Estate, that
there was little more than Ignorance, Captivity and Barba-
rifme amongst them, I did not
think fit to insist there; since,
however their wits might be
as excellent now as in former
times, they seemed to want
not only the Means which
might enable them to find out
any Learned Truth, but even
the

the heart to believe it. Neither did their Ancient or almoſt univerſally taught Religion (being *Ethnick* and *Pagan*) any way affect me there, or in any Country elſe : ſince being now intermitted, and diſcontinued for many Ages, I could not but think it built in great part upon weak and uncertain Principles, more eſpecially in thoſe Points, which are now wholly antiquated and aboliſhed.

From hence therefore I caſt mine Eye upon *Italy* ; as the Country wherein, not only all the Ancient Learning of the *Greeks*, but alſo of the *Romans*, was carefully preſerved and taught ; But as here again I found almoſt all they produced in point of Religion to be controvert-

troverted among other Nations
in *Europe*, with muchacrimonie
and Bitterneſs; and that beſides
among the ſeveral Opinions and
Sects the ſubſequent times have
brought forth, the latter for
the moſt part have diſſented
more from them than the former; inſomuch that the *Puri-
tan* hath departed more from
them than the *Proteſtant*, and
the *Proteſtant* than the *Luthe-
ran*; I could not ſo ſafely rely
upon them, as not to enquire,
why the Tenents of the *Church*
of *Rome* are ſo much deſerted?
But as here again I found my
ſelf intangled in Controverſies,
I thought fit to make a pauſe
before I engaged my ſelf too
far in thoſe Tumultuous and
uncharitable Diſputes. And the
rather, becauſe I found that
even

even the knowledge of the different Sects of Christian Religion alone, took up more time in the study of them than I could possibly hope to obtain, altho' I should live beyond the ordinary age of man; so that whereas I thought my self obliged for the discharge of my Conscience to study not only all Religions that have been or are in the World, I found the *Romanish* Religion in its divers Sects alone of greater Intricacie, than that I could by any Reason or Authority dissolve or unty the many Scruples or Knots in them: since flying somtimes from *Reason* to *Faith*, and then again from *Faith* to *Reason*, with a singular agility in both, I found my self unable to follow them in any

any one certain way. I confess,
that if they had adhered singly
to either of these two. nothing
could have scandalized me;
since that which was delivered
upon *Reason,* I should have examined, and finally accepted
upon the same ground: and as
well, should I have believed
those Points of *Faith,* which
were delivered me upon the
Reverend Authority of the
Church; especially, when it
could have been proved, that
any former *Church* or *Congre-*
gation had under their hands and
Seals, or in any other Authen-
tick manner subscribed, as eye-
Witnesses to that they consign'd
unto Posterity, and not as
Hearers only; it being of great
moment in the affirmation of
things past, to set down what
they

they knew certainly, and to
come afterwards to what was
told them by others, which
they again had from others, and
so perhaps from many descents;
especially, if such things were
related, as neither they from
whom they heard it, nor indeed any mortal man by Natural Means could know. Neither would it be sufficient to
say, that their *Knowledge* was
Supernatural or *Divine*, since as
that is more than could be
known in following times, so,
when it were granted, it would
inferr little to me, but that
which I would believe without it. For if any under the
name of a *Prophet* should bid
me do a Sin, or be Impenitent
for Sins done, I should not believe him, though he pretended

a thoufand *Revelations* for it:
And on the other fide, if he bid
me be Vertuous and Penitent,
though he had not any fhadow
of *Revelation* for it, I fhould
give entire Credit to him.

The Validity of Revelation proved by its Doctrine.

That therefore the Certainty
of that Doctrine, which is called
Revealed, or the word of God
in any Age or Country, comes
not to me fimply either from
the Authority of him that faid
the holy Spirit did fo dictate
the word to him: No, nor
from the Authority of them
that believed it: (how many or
great foever:) but from the
Goodnefs of the Doctrine it felf;
without which, I fhould believe
                                    but

but little in any extraordinary kind. Every man, in what Age or Country, that teacheth goodnefs, fpeaks the word of God to me; and if the Contrary, he fhall never make me believe, he knoweth God, or heard him fpeak fo much as one fyllable, much lefs that he is fo familiar with God, as to know him by his Voice.

Four feveral kinds of Revelations.

The Learned *Toftatus* mentions four feveral ways whereby God is faid to have made Revelations in former times; as for Example: *Firft,* when God and his Angels affumed a vifible fhape, as when he appeared to *Gideon, Judg.* 6. and to *Manoah* and his Wife, *Judg.* 13. Secondly,

condly, When he was not seen, but only heard, as *Numb.* 7. and when he called *Samuel,* 1 *Sam.* 3. *Thirdly,* When he wrought only upon the Imaginations of men, sleeping or waking; as when God told *Abimelech* in a *Dream,* that he was a dead man, for taking away another mans Wife, *Gen.* 20.   *Fourthly,* and *lastly,* When God raiseth the Understanding · to know those things which otherwise he could not know, either by a kind of Extasie, or without; and of this kind was *Paul's* rapture into the *third Heavens;* at which time it may be doubtful whether the Soul remained in the Body or no.

Having thus now recited his several kinds of *Revelations,* it will be necessary in the next place

place to enquire, whether there might not be Fallacies in all these ways? And when there was no Fallacy, whether their Proof was not only by single Witnesses? The *Popiſh Clergie* (in ſuch a caſe) will tell us, That we muſt believe reverently of things delivered to us in *Holy Writ*, for that they have neither Errour nor Fraud in them: And if that does not ſatisfie you, they will then tell you, you muſt come to them for a further Anſwer: Not conſidering, that if the *Gentiles* ſhould require the ſame credit to be given to their *Revelations* upon their own ſingle Teſtimony, how we ſhould do to ſhake them off: the ſame Reaſon lying for us to believe the one, as the other, both equally depending on *Faith*.   A

A Dialogue concerning Revelations.

Therefore in the first place, I should demand in a Rational and Judicial way, how I could be assured, that the Priests *had received a* Revelation; *and what was the time, place, and manner thereof? In Answer to which, I conceive the* Priests *would tell me; That* Laicks *ought not further to enquire into such* Mysteries *than becomes them; that if this their* Revelation *were not accepted as an unquestionable and necessary* Truth, *there could be no cause thereof, but an* obdurate heart, *and want of* Divine Grace *in me; that if the* Sacerdotal *word might not be taken concerning the* Truth *of the said* Revelation.*

lation, *there was no other way to inform me thereof: It being* Gods *manner to speak to his beloved Servants, and not to such gross* Sinners *as I was; and to be* brief, *that if I did not give entire credit to this* Revelation *of theirs, it was for want of* Faith: *And therefore, that no better counsel could be given me, than to pray that all obstructions might be taken away, and instead of my* heart of stone, *that I might receive an* heart of flesh, *such as may be capable of this* heavenly Illumination. Finally, *They would reply nothing concerning the* time or manner *of their* Revelation, *but only in general say, that the* Place was God's holy Temple, *where none could be partakers of the* Word of God, *but such only as were*

his

his near Servants, and did or-
dinarily take their rest and sleep
therein.

Now to this I should Answer,
That if I might not know the
time *and* manner, *when and how*
this their Revelation *was made,*
I would yet gladly be informed,
what Language *was used betwixt*
them, and whether the words
were of God's immediate invention, *or that there were only cer-*
tain Notes *and* Characters *in*
use betwixt them, whereby they
understood one another? Or o-
therwise, if they had not a par-
ticular Language *betwixt them,*
which was intelligible; whether
God *spake the ordinary* Language *of that* Country *, and in*
what Tone; *whether the same*
were lowder *than* Thunder, *or*
only the ordinary heighth, *or*
whether

whether lower yet, by some close
secret expression, somewhat
less than a whisper? To which
I believe the Priests would Reply, That if a King or Principal Magistrate did send me a
Message or Command by some
one of his known Officers, I
would not then presume to make
all these Questions, they being
not only uncivil, but also impertinent and derogatory to the Supreme Authority, and therefore that they who were known
Ministers of God, did, without giving further account, require Obedience from me in his Name. But
notwithstanding all this, I should
yet take the boldness to ask
them, (supposing they heard such
words) how yet they could know
that God spake them, and whether they were so familiar with
the

the perſon of that God, *as to know him by his* Voice, *and diſtinguiſh him from all others?* How they could aſſure themſelves firmly, that it was no inferiour Spirit *that gave them this* Revelation, *there being* Spirits *of both ſorts, both* good *and* bad, *which uſe to deliver* Oracles *and* Revelations, *according to the* Doctrine *of the* Manichees, *who founded their Opinions upon that ſentence,* viz. that the Devil is the God of this world. *But again, ſuppoſing it was a* good Spirit *that ſpoke, whether* Camillus, *or his* Boy *who waited on him in the* Temple, *did hear or underſtand the* Voice *as well as himſelf?* Here I know the Prieſts Anſwer *would be, That neither himſelf, nor any elſe could come to the knowledge of* God's *Will, but*

by

their means and conveyance:
nd for the rest would again re-
ire my Obedience, on peril of
being condemn'd as an Infidel;
inking by these words at least
overawe me.

But this would be so far from
rifying me, that it would but
t into my head more Scruples,
cerning the Truth of their
velation? when pursuing my
sy, I should gladly demand of
, how yet I could be assured,
at in the repeating of this their
racle or Revelation, *they had*
itted no part thereof through
getfulness; or added any thing
it by a Paraphrase, *or* Ex-
cation; And briefly, whether
thing were interweaved or
aged thertin?

The Priests *would here assu-*
dly reply, That it was but a
pro-

*prophane part in me to doubt any
thing were either added to, or taken from the* Divine Revelation,
*much less any thing mixed or in-
terwoven with it : and that the
same* God, *who gave them this*
Revelation, *did and would pre-
serve it entire in their memory;
for further proof whereof, they
were ready to set it down, and
sign it under their Hands and
Seals, that so it might be trans-
mitted to* Posterity, *as an* Au-
thentick Record : *To which also,
the* Amanuenses *or* Coppiers *of
it might repair to correct all
that should be depraved, either
by their carelesness, or wilful
perversion of the Sense thereof,
that so their Errors might afterwards be rectified, attested and
subscribed by sufficient* Witnesses, *as agreeing with the* Original :

ral; *there being no other Means
so good to ascertain us* Laicks,
*that nothing therein was counter-
feit,* &c. *Which* Method *(I confess) if it had been used in all*
Ages *and* Countries *where* Revelations *are said to have been
made in private to* Priests, *would
have been much approved; since*
Copies *of* Copies, *through many*
Descents, *may be subject to many*
Corruptions, *especially among
those who would draw all things
to their own* Interest; *which
might as well have become these
latter Times, as the former; since
our Modern* Priests *(for the most
part) turn* Religion *into* Faction,
*striving to render all others of
different Perswasions (though in
the least matters) odious. Which*
Bitterness *of* Spirit *we find not
evidently remarked among the*

C   Heathen

Heathen Priests ; *fo that how Ignorant and Falfe foever they were, yet are they not recorded to have been* Incendiaries , *and* Perfecutors *of one another even unto* Death , *for* Religion *and* Confcience *fake :* No, they had no fuch hellifh *Contrivances as the* Parifian *and* Hibernian Maffacres ; *no fuch Inftruments of the* Devil, *as* Ravilliac, Clement, *and the* Prieft *that poyfon'd our* English Monarch *in the* Eucharift ; *no fuch* Traiterous Confpiracies *as the* Powder-plot : *Nor did they ufe to convert one another to their Opinions by* Fire *and* Fagot, *and* Rofting Kings *alive, as the* Spaniards *did in the* Indies. *He that compares but the Behaviour of thofe of the Religious among the* Heathens, *with the Carriage of our* Popifh Bifhops

here

here *in* England *before the* Refor-
mation, *as related by our own*
Chriſtian *Writers, would take the*
Heathen Prieſts *for much the*
better Chriſtians *of the two.*

So that, notwithſtanding all
this, I ſhould not give the Prieſts
over ſo, but at leaſt tell them, I
could have wiſhed they had proceeded more clearly with me; ſince
the more they debaſed my Under-
ſtanding in Divine Myſteries,
the more was I obliged to ſtand to
my Common Reaſon, until they
had made all things manifeſt or
intelligible to me, without going
about to convince me of Infideli-
ty, becauſe I believed not more
than I underſtood: or when a
further Belief were required, I
hoped they would not charge me to
believe it any otherwiſe than as a
thing poſſible, or at moſt but like-

ly, since this was all I could do, when God had given me no suffi- cient Revelation *for the confirm- ing of theirs.   And to affirm it a good Plea in the* Court of Hea- ven, *to say, That a Man began at the* Faith *that was taught in his* Native Country ; *Who might not then excuse himself for adhering to the* grossest Superstition *that can be imagined in any* Age *or* Country *whatever, where no less Esteem and Veneration was given publickly to their* Sacerdotal Col- lege, *than is now paid to the pre- sent* Church of Rome *in* Italy *and* Spain.   Finally, therefore, I should ask them, How any* Priest *could assure and satisfie my Con- science, that the* Revelation *made to him did so concern me, that I must embrace it as an undoubted* Axiom, *or* Truth ? *To which (I*

am

am confident) *they would anſwer,*
as formerly, That they had diſ-
charged their Duty in delivering
Gods Word, *and that I ought to*
take heed leſt I be ſeverely pu-
niſhed for want of Faith, *and ſo*
leave me, after having with much
gravity *expreſſed their* ſorrow
for my incorrigible ſtubborn
Heart, &c.

But, notwithſtanding all this,
I do not yet deny, but that *Re-*
velations may be made to Men
either *ſleeping* or *waking;* but
where, I ſuppoſe, (as we find in
Holy Writ) earneſt *Prayers* have
been made before-hand, and
ſome *publick* and *miraculous Con-*
firmation of the thing *revealed*
hath followed. However, unleſs the thing in it ſelf be right
good and *honeſt,*I ſhould not conceive it was *God* that ſpake, but

some *Evil Spirit* that would deceive me ; it having pleased God so to implant the Love of *Goodness* and *Truth* in the *Soul*, that he hath made them a part of *Common Reason*, and consp̄cuous by their own *Light* ; from which therefore if we recede, we shall find our selves cast not onely into much Errour and Darkness, but even in the Court of our own *Consciences* criminal and condemned : For which Cause also I believe *God* is so sparing in making publick *Relations*, because if Men did wholly trust to them, it might be a means of making them neglect their proper Duties. *It would be* (as the Learned *Gregory* in his *Posthuma* observes) *a Stumbling-block to the* Gentiles, *when they found it read in* Osea,

that

that God *commanded* a Prophet *to commit Adultery:* and in Exodus, *that he taught his own People how to cozen the* Egyptians: *How could they believe* (saith he) *that there was* no God *like the* God *of the* Hebrews, *when they should find in the Scriptures, that even this* God *had also a* Right-hand *and a* Son ? *Or that if he had been so much better than those of the* Heathen, *was it likely that* Aaron *his own* High Priest, *would have preferred their* Apis *or* Egyptian Calf *before him ?* But the Reason of all this is, because to *unenlightned Nature* these Passages might seem inconsistent with the Attributes of the *Deus Optimus Maximus;* and for that (as our aforesaid Learned Author well notes) *all ways of* Religion *would seem*

C. 4. *strange,*

strange, but that we are taught betimes to fear: and till we receive a Spirit of Judgment to discern the Right way, every Way is thought to be Wrong, but that which we are brought up in. And thus much for *Publick Revelations.*

Of Visions and Apparitions.

Now if any Man should say a *Vision* appear'd to him, I should believe him as far as it was fit to credit a *single Witness* in so rare a Case ; but certainly I should not depart from my *Common Reason,* whatsoever he should pretend to teach upon those Grounds ; and from *single Witnesses,* and no more, the greatest *Miracles* in all Vulgar Superstitions are mostly derived, as

would

would appear to any one that should look back from *Age* to *Age*, to the Original of all such *wonderful Narrations:* Or, if more Perfons than one are faid at firft to have concurred in the Relation, it ought again to be confidered, whether they that would eftablifh it did not acquire much *Authority*, and procure many Advantages thereby unto themfelves; and that either of *Honour*, or *Riches*, the one being as prevalent with the *Vain-glorious*, as the other with the *Covetous?* The *Nature* of Men being for the moft part prone always to entertain fuch *Beliefs* as turn to their own Benefit.

C 5 *Tefti-*

Teftimonies Weak.

Furthermore, in my Opinion it is to be obferved, That as it is not fafe to truft abfolutely to any *fingle* or *weak Teftimony* in Matters of great Confequence; fo will it be much more dange-rous to frame new *Doctrines* or *Conclufions* out of them, for di-recting of our felves in the whole Courfe of our Life; fince *Errour* may be thus multiplied without end.

Of Miracles.

Thefe *Confiderations* therefore brought me at laft to be more fparing in the Belief of *Miracu-lous Narrations*, and efpecially for the Building any new *Do-*

Ctrines

ftrines upon them; fince *Im-poftors*, fuch as *Jannes* and *Jam-bres*, have been faid to do *Mira-cles*, whofe *Egyptian Doctrines* I yet fhould never believe. I might fay fomething alfo of *Apollonius Tyanæus* and *Simon Magus*, who (however they may be believed to have done *Mira-cles*) did yet not teach any *Uni-verfal Doctrine*, to which Affent was given. Neither fhall I in-fift upon the little Credit given heretofore to the feigned *Mira-cles* or *Revelations* by *Pagan Priefts* among the more Judici-ous fort of the *Gentiles.*

Wherefore, it is no good Ar-gument to fay, *That fuch a Man did* Miracles, *and therefore I be-lieve all he faith:* Since thofe things may feem *Miraculous* to my weak Capacity, which appear

pear not fo to wifer Men. Be-
fides, things may be done by
Natural Means, which fome may
miftake for *Miracles* and *Conju-
ration*; as all Books of *Chymi-
ſtry* and *Natural Philofophy* can
teſtifie : *And upon this* Vulgar
Ignorance *it is* (faith *Monſieur
Naudæus,* in his Treatife of *Ma-
gick*) *that the moſt Ingenious and
Learnedeſt Men in the World
have been defamed as* Conjurers
and Wizards, *becauſe their Ac-
cuſers were* Fools *and* Blockheads.
Again, by *Confederacy,* where
one helps the other to abufe the
People ; of which kind, Examples have been frequent, and fo
well known, that I fhall omit
troubling my Reader or my
felf with them in fo fmall a
Treatiſe.

Of

Of Prophecy and Prophets.

In like manner should their pretended *Prophecies* draw me as little to any *New Religion*; since one shall hardly meet with a *Prophecy* delivered so clearly and so perspicuously, as to mark out and distinguish from all others any Person or Event in subsequent Times. For my part, as I could never yet esteem any thing to be an undoubted *Prophecy*, which in the first place was not like a *Picture*, (wherein it is not enough to describe or Paint one Member or Part of the Face or Body, unless the Symetry and other Parts were together represented with the outward Stature, Colour, and Fashion:) so likewise I should not much

much regard the Exterior Form,
if his Actions were not reprefented to future Times in fuch
manner, as the *Prophecy* might
be like an *History*, wherein it is
required that the *Time*, *Place*,
and *Manner* of all his Actions
fhould be defcribed fo particular-
ly, as to diftinguifh the whole
Courfe of his Life from all o-
thers. And that therefore many of the doubtful and obfcure
Predictions that have been at-
tributed to divers, who from
thence have acquired the Names
of *Prophets*, feem to be little
more than bold Conjectures,
which might in fome Age or
other take its Events : there being nothing, I will not fay,
likely or *poffible*, but even *un-*
likely, and onely not *impoffible*,
that in fome *Time*, *Place*, or *Man-*

ner will not have its Effect and Fulfilling. Wherefore, if any Man hath undertaken heretofore, or fhall yet in this Age undertake to *Prophefie*, upon what vain ground foever, yet if he. get that Credit among future Ages as to be thought a *Prophet*, he will find thofe that fhall apply his Words to fome Action or Event that did or will (in all likelihood) follow ; which Motives made me as doubtful of their *Prophecies*, as of fuch *Miracles* and *Revelations* I formerly mentioned. *Obfopæus* is faid to have put forth Books which fpake plainer of *Chrift*, than the *Prophets* of the *Old Teftament* did ; which our Learned *Criticks* have neverthelefs rejected as *fpurious*.

The *Heavenly Bodies* had outward

ward Worſhip given them from the Excellency of their Natures; but the *Heathen Prieſts* had their chief Credit from their *Prophecies* and *Prediction*: who contented not themſelves with the perſwading the People that they had *Revelations*, unleſs they could perſwade them further, that they could foretel things to come, and ſo acquire to themſelves the Name of *Prophets.* The manner of *Prediction* among the *Jews* was by *Dreams*, *Urim*, or *Prophets*; and *Saul's* throwing off his Clothes, lying naked upon the Ground a Day and a Night, and ſo Propheſied, 1 *Sam.* 19. and by the *Witch* of *Endor*, to whom *Saul* had recourſe in his Extremities, who deſired her to raiſe up *Samuel* to him, which ſhe doing,

Samuel

Samuel appeared, and told *Saul*
what fhould follow, 1 *Sam.* 28.
The *Urim* and *Thummim* were
two Precious Stones fo called,
the one *Light* , and the other
Truth or *Integrity* ; the one an
Onyx or *Sardonix*, and the other
an *Emrald* ; out of the vibrati-
on of whofe Beauty, *Oracles* and
Prophecies were called and ut-
ter'd : In imitation whereof, the
Devil and *Kelly* together delu-
ded old *Dr. Dee* with their *An-
gelical Stone* (as they called it)
in *Queen Elizabeths* time ; if you
will give Credit to the Record
thereof, preferved in the famous
*Cottonian Library,*and fince pub-
lifhed in Print by *Dr. Cafaubon.*
Varro faith, That the *Ancient
Priefts* of *Egypt* (who were alfo
Judges) wore upon their Necks
a great *Emrald* , called *Truth.*

Some

Some of the *Rabbins* attribute not so much to the *Stones*, as to certain Writings under them.

Judgments made of future Events by remarquing the Configurations and Operations of the *Planets* and *Stars*, as also *Predictions* made from *Natural Causes*, are, without all question, not onely lawful, but commendable, although of little certainty: But the cunning *Artists*, the *Priests*, who in *Egypt* were anciently *Astrologers*, used to mingle with their *Divinations*, *Lies* of their own Invention, whereby they acquired more than by their *Truths*. The word for *Divinations* in general is *Mantike*, which *Plato* in *Phædri* derives from *Munike*, signifying *furious* or *mad*.

The difference between *Prophets*,

bers, and those that were in
Ecstasies or *Trances*, was this :
The *Prophets* were said to run
up and down raging and crying,
whereas the *Extatekoi* appear-
ing devoid of *Sense* and Understanding, seem'd little less than
dead, till they awaked out of
their *Trances*; wherein also they
remained so long, that they had
time enough to devise something which might delude the
people. By this kind of *Impo-
sture, Mahomet* did often prevail,
when he arose from his *Fits* of
the *Falling Sickness.* Also from
these sorts of *Raptures* anciont-
ly it may be supposed the *Ethnick* Narration of the *Elyzian
Fields*, and their *Separate State
f Souls after Death*, together
with their manner of *Reward
nd Punishment*, were at first
devised,

devifed, and then vented to the
People. Neither have the *Chri-*
ftian Times been without fuch
Saints, (I mean not the true and
holy ones:) but fome that pre-
tending to *Sanctity,* have in their
Ecftafies (whether counterfeit
or not) feigned that they had
feen *Souls* in *Purgatory ;* whereof the *Legend* will inform you
more.

Neverthelefs, It is obferved,
that the *Souls* of Men, having
many more *Faculties* than what
the Reprefentation of Worldly
Objects can excite or call up,
and fometimes freeing themfelves from their ufual Employ-
ments, and the Objects they
meet with in this Life, afcend to
the *Contemplation* and even *Vi-*
fion of *Divine Objects,* making
themfelves thus capable of
know-

knowing not onely things paſt, but thoſe that are to come : to which kind of *Ecſtaſie*, whether *St. Paul's Rapture* into the *third Heavens* may be referred, I leave to others to judge. In like manner, we read of divers ſtrange and incredible *Ecſtaſies* that have hapned to Men in this kind : as (not to mention our Modern *Voyages*, which ſpeak of *Indians* that in their *Trances* will diſcover what Ships are coming to their *Iſlands*, and from what *Ports*, many Months before their Arrival ;) the like hapned of old to *Pamphilus* the Son of *Neocles*, who (as *Plato* ſaith) lay ten days in a *Trance*, and afterwards told Wonders. But to credit theſe things is altogether matter of *Faith*, and not of *Common Reaſon* ; from whence

I

I cannot recede, or build any
new *Doctrine* upon such Re-
ports ; especially, when there is
no Divine Authority like the
Scriptures for it, nor Original
Attestation, that the *Prophecy*
was consigned unto us in those
very Words wherein they are
now extant ; and for the rest,
that they are more obscure than
that an unquestionable Certainty may be built upon them.
But herein I am content to let
every Man use his own Judgment, and therefore shall quit
this Subject with one Observa-
tion, which is, That by reading
Mother Shiptons Prophecies when
we are *Boys*, we do the better
rellish *Nostredamus* when we
are Men : especially since every
vain-glorious *Expositor* of such
Prophecies looks upon himself

as

as little lefs than a *Minor-Pro-phet.*

Now All thefe Points having been for a long time debated and examined by me, to the beft of my Underftanding, I did think fit the rather to ftudy and inquire out thofe *Common Princi-ples* of *Religion* I could any where meet with; onely before I undertook this great Task, I thought it not amifs to advife upon what Grounds the Controverted Points amongft them did move. But, as here I obferved nothing but matter of *Faith* , or *Belief* concerning Things paft, queftioned in any Age or Country ; fo did I the more eafily pafs by it, to come to thofe *Articles* which were grounded not onely upon *Rea-fon* and *Univerfal Confent* of *Re-ligions,*

ligions, but are (I believe) extant and operative in the Hearts
of all Men, which are not pre-
poſſeſs'd and obſtructed with
erroneous *Doctrines*, and (I am
ſure) moſt deeply engraven in
mine. Which being done, I
thought it my Duty to inquire,
Whether by an apt Connexion
of the Parts thereof, I might fix
ſo ſolid a Foundation, that I
might repoſe thereon, as the
firſt and principal Ground of all
Religious Worſhip.

The *Articles* which I propoſe,
are *Five* in number; and the
ſame which the great Oracle
and Commander of his Time,
for Wit, Learning, and Courage,
tam Marti quam Mercurio, the
the *Lord Herbert, Baron of Cher-
bury*, delivered; and which (I
am confident) are ſo *Catholique*

of

or *Universal*, that all the *Religions* that ever were, are, or (I believe) ever shall be, did, do, and will embrace them. The *Articles* are these.

The Five Catholick or Universal Articles of Religion.

I. *That there is One onely Supreme God.*

II. *That He chiefly is to be Worshipped.*

III. *That Vertue, Goodness, and Piety, accompanied with Faith in, and Love to God, are the best ways of Worshipping Him.*

IV. *That we should repent of our Sins from the bottom of our Hearts, and turn to the Right Way.*

V. And lastly, *That there is*

D a

a Reward and Punishment after this Life.

Now of each of these in particular.

First Article, Of One God.

As to the First Article: Tho divers *Godheads* or *Divine Natures* were celebrated or worshipped in several Ages or Countries throughout the World, yet there is no Agreement or Consent, but onely concerning *One Supreme God,* under the *Attributes* of *Optimus* and *Maximus;* the one supposing his *Providence,* the other his *Power,* in the highest degree and extention: and both these together inferring his *Wisdom, Justice, Mercy,* and the rest. Thus the

the *Heathens* beſtowed ſeveral Names upon the *Deity*, accord- ing to the ſeveral Parts of the *Univerſe*; calling him, in the Starry Heaven and *Æther*, *Ju- piter*; in the Air, *Juno*; in the Winds, *Æolus*; in the Sea, *Nep- tune*; in the Earth and Subter- raneous Parts, *Pluto*; in Learn- ing, Knowledge, and Invention, *Mercury*, *Minerva*, and the *Mu- ſes*; in War, *Mars*; in Pleaſure, *Venus*; in Corn and the Pro- duction of Fruits of the Earth, *Ceres*; in Wine, *Bacchus*; and the like. Under which ſeveral Appellations were ſignified one- ly the various Operations of the *One Immenſe God:* which makes *Minutius* well obſerve, That *Qui Jovem principem volant, fal- luntur in nomine, ſed de una Pote- ſtate conſentiunt.*

Second Article, That God is to be
Worshipped.

As to the Second Article;
Tho divers other *Deities, God-*
heads, or *Divine Natures,* have
been celebrated or worshipped
more or less, in some inferiour
or subordinate kind ; yet there
is no *Agreement* or *Universal*
Consent concerning the *Worship*
of any other than the *Supreme*
God ; in whom, Authors generally say, all other *Godheads* or
Divine Natures are *worshipped.*

Third Article, How God is to be
Worshipped.

As to the *Third Article:* Tho
divers *Rites, Mysteries,* and *Sa-*
cra's, (as the *Romans* call them)
were

were introduced to the *Worſhip* of the *Supreme God*; yet that there is no Univerſal Conſent or Agreement concerning them, but that a pure and untainted Mind, (as being conſcious in it ſelf of no Unworthineſs) toge-ther with a Virtuous and Pious Life, (teſtified by the Expreſſi-ons of Goodneſs and Charity to all Men) and accompanied with *Love*, *Faith*, and *Hope* in *God*, were undoubted ways of Ser-ving him: *ſit pura mente colen-dus.* The Ancient *Jews* and Modern *Chriſtians* have many *Rites* and *Ceremonies* common with the *Gentiles*; which is more than vulgar *Divines* do ima-gine. Moſt of the *Jewiſh Laws* and *Rites* were practiſed indif-ferently among the *Heathens*, or at leaſt did not much vary

D 3   from

from them, as the diligent Searchers into *Antiquity* well know. The *Gentiles*, as well as the *Jews*, held the most substantial Parts of *Moses* his Doctrine, without differing in much more than certain particular Laws, more proper for that Country than any other; as, their not eating *Swines Flesh*, and making *Adultery Death*. If it be said, That that Precept in the *Decalogue* (against *Graven Images*) was particular to the *Jews*; It will be found a Mistake: for that the *Persians*, and otheir neighbouring Nations, concurred therein, as well as the *Jews*; as also in most of their other *Commandments*: Thus *Feriari Deo* is accounted a kind of keeping a *Sabboth, &c.* amongst the *Heathens*: And *St. Austin* (*lib.* 20. *ch.* 19.

ch. 19. against *Faustus*) faith, That the *Gentiles* were not so grievously lapsed into the Worship of *False Gods*, but that they retained the Opinion of *One True God*, from whom every Nature whatsoever is derived. *Finally*, Whatsoever tends to Mans Perfection, is eminently and primarily in *God* : But the *Notions* of *Providence*, *Wisdom*, *Justice*, *Mercy*, *Love*, &c. tend to his Perfection ; *Ergo*, Hence the *Gentiles* took their Rise from themselves, as believing that they were *Gods Children*, and made after his *Image*.

Fourth Article, Of Repentance and Sacrifices.

As to the Fourth Article : Tho *Sacrifices* for the abolishing

D 4 of

of Sin of more than one fort,
as alfo *Expiations* , *Luftrations*,
and divers other *Rites* invented
by the *Sacerdotal Order*, were
ufed for the *purging* of Men from
Sin ; yet was there no *Univerfal
Confent* or Agreement concerning them. But that *Repentance*
is a certain Sign of *Gods Spirit*
working in us, and the onely Re-
medy for Sin that is declared
publickly to all Mankind, and
the moft rational way to return
to *God* and *Vertue*, is by Univerfal Confent eftablifhed every
where, without fo much as the
leaft Contradiction. Not that
I think *God's* Juftice can be fa-
tisfied by meer *Repentance*, and
turning to a good Life ; but
that a further *Satisfaction* or *Re-
paration* for our Offences againft
the *Divine Majefty* is required.
Yet

Yet as there is no Univerſal Agreement concerning the Means how this is effected, (it being of greater Scrutiny than Mans Reaſon can attain unto) ſo I ſhall in part wave this Diſcourſe; and the rather, for that many do not ſee why (according to the ordinary Rules of Juſtice) God ſhould puniſh one Man for the Sins of another : or, to go further, for that Frailty of our own Nature, which without our Conſent was beſtowed upon us? To which, give me leave to add theſe few Remarques. 1. *Decipimur ſpecie recti:* We have not a true Judgment of *Of Good and Evil.* Good and Bad; eſteeming many things Evil, which in themſelves are not ſo. An Hiſtory drawn in a Picture may

D 5 have

have in it Reprefentations of Battels, Slaughters, Drunkards, Harlots, and Firing of Cities, Shipwracks, or the like ; and yet may be as lovely a Piece of Painting, as if it reprefented an *Affembly* of *Divines* : And fo, perhaps, in a Natural Confideration, may be thought an Age that produces fuch Actions, as well as if it brought forth none but Examples of *Vertue.* 2. We denominate *Good* and *Evil* onely from our particular Intereft ; fo that perhaps our *Vertues* may prove but *Falfe Money*, of no *intrinfick Value*, although it bear the Stamp of our Approbation upon it. 3. A Well-being is the primary Appetite of Nature in all things ; and fo as we judge any thing more or lefs agreeing or contrary thereto,

to, fo are we more or lefs incli-
ning or averfe thereto: where-
upon our Will, either for or
againſt any thing. to do or for-
bear any thing, doth always
follow our Judgment; which
Judgment is framed by feveral
things, *viz.* the Temper of our
Brain, & our Education, together
with the various Encounters,
Succeſſes, and Experiments in
the Courſe of our Lives: all
which (it is manifeſt) are not in
our own power, but proceeds
from the Temper of our Pa-
rents, the Diet, Climate, and
Cuſtoms of our Country, with
diverſity of Occurrents and
Conjunctures of the Times;
which are produced with op-
portune Interventions of one
another, in a continued *Series* of
God's Providence in the difpofal
of,

of them, and of such *Idea's* as he thereby sets before our Fanfie. 'Tis apparent that he does thereby lead and guide all our Thoughts, Words, and

*Of Predesti-
nation and
Free will.* Actions; yet not by any violent Protrusion, but by our own Consent, either by way of Delight, or as to the lesser Evil; and ever by Opinion, whether true or erroneous. So that our Consent not being violated, but led on by our own Choice, we justly become liable to Praise or Blame, and yet are in all our Ways under the Infallible Conduct of God. 4. As our *Body* is a Portion of the *Body* of the *World*, so is our *Spirit*, which guides and acts us, a *Beam* of the *Spirit* of *God* ; which also, tho in its own Nature clear, yet is

that

hat Clearneſs in us more or
leſs, according to our Temper
whereinto it ſhines : Thus we
find our ſelves of different Fan-
cies, when we are Phlegmatick,
or when our Blood is Black and
Groſs, from what we are when
our Blood and Brain is Pure and
Thin ; and accordingly our
Judgment grows more or leſs
perſpicacious and rectified ; and
by conſequence the Inclinati-
ons of our Will better or worſe :
yet therein no violence is offer'd us. *Spiritus in Nobis non*
manet in Identitate, ſed recens
ingeritur, per renovationem con-
tinuam, ſicut flamma, ſed veloci-
re tranſitu, quia res eſt ſpiritua-
lior. Nos enim quotidie facti
ſumus ex iis quæ tranſeunt in nos :
morimur & renaſcimur quotidie,
neque iidem hodie & heri ſumus :
&

& perfonam quam tranfeunte
non fentimus, tandem pertranfi
agnofcimus.   Nulla eft autem re
rum tranfitio in nos nifi per via
Alimenti: Omne Alimentum re
fpectu Alimentandi eft confimile &
debilius :   Alimentantis corpus
fuccrefcit nobis in corpus; fpiritus
in fpiritu: non tamen . proportio
utriufque fit nobis ad proportionem
cibi & potus, aut aeris, nifi a nobis
bene fuperantur; aliter etenim non
alunt, ingefta, fed opprimunt fi
fortiora funt, corrumpunt fi diffi.
milia, idque plus minufve pro gra-
du in utroque: Ideoque quo melius
res · procedat multa fieri oportet:
primum prudens electio & mode-
ratio eorum, quæ ingerenda funt;
& deinceps debita præparatio
per artem, ut nobis fimiliora &
debiliora fiant : ex parte noftri
præcipuum eft exercitium fre
quens,

xens, sed modicum, quo calor na-
uralis vigeat. Again, The Al-
teration of our Judgment from
outward Occurrences is also of
great importance to present us
with new *Idea's*, which divert
us this way or that way, and so
into Mischief or Preservation,
yet always by our own *election*:
As for example, A Man going
to *London*, perhaps finding the
way dirty, leaves it, and takes
into a Bie way, whereby he mis-
ses *Thieves*, who were then on
the *Road*, although he knew not
of them ; or, perhaps, lights
upon another Mischance in this
Way, which he had missed in
the other: Here is *God's Conduct*
of him, either to his *Good* or
Harm, leading him by that
Idea of avoiding Dirt, yet without *Compulsion*, and by his *Free*
Election:

Election ; wherefore he cannot complain but of himself: Yet *God* did undoubtedly from all Eternity both *foresee* and *decree* this *Election*, with the Event which should follow thereon. For thus *God* doth ever manage us by the Temper of our *Body*, with his inoperating Spirit therein ; and by meeting us from without in such Encounters and Occurrences, as will infallibly carry us by our own *Choice* into such things as from all Eternity he had ordained.

5. Some will here object, That if God gives us to *will* or to *refuse*, and that it were not in our own *power* to *will* or to *refuse*, then how could we be praised or punished for. ought we *do*, or neglect to *do* ? To which I answer, Just as well as it befals us

for

for having *Flesh* and *Blood*:
Our having *Flesh* and *Blood*
makes us subject to much *Pain*
and *Pleasure*; and yet this our
Body of *Flesh* and *Blood* was
given us of *God*, when we had
no power to refuse it: And if
we put our Finger or any Li-
ving Creature by force into the
Fire, it will smart and suffer as
much, as if it had gone in by
its own desire; for the ground
of its *suffering* is not in the being *willing*, or *unwilling*, but in
its *disagreeableness* to *Fire*. And
so when a Man takes into de-
bauched intemperate Courses,
he falls into Diseases; and whether God or himself drive him,
that is not the Point; the true
Cause is, the venomous and op-
pressive Humours which by
these Courses he puts into his
Body,

Body, deftructive to its own
Nature. 6. *And laftly*, It was
well faid of one, who having
contrived and put in execution
a great and politick Bufinefs,
and being asked, Whether it was
his own Care, or Divine Providence, that had brought this
great Work to pafs? he replied,
Fuit certo Providentia Divina,
fed quæ per me tranfiit. For if
we fhould fee a *Sun-beam* in at a
Hole enlightning a *dark Room*,
'twould be a very fhallow Con-
ception, to fuppofe that this
Beam did move or enlighten
one way or other, otherwife
than as it felf was continually
enlightned and carried about
by its *Original* the *Sun*, from
whom it can never be feparated,
nor have any Vertue apart:
And the very fame Relation

and Condition. has each particular Man's *Spirit* with the
Spirit of God. *Dei opus sumus
nos parentibus instrumentis; acti-
onesque nostræ Dei sunt opera instrumentis nobis, sed per electio-
nem nostram agentibus : Ista vero
electio per aptas conjuncturas &
Ideas adeo inemissas invitatur &
regitur: ideoque nos Creaturæ
sumus momentaneæ æterni Dei
apparitiones, quas tantum terris
ostendunt fata, nec ultra esse si-
nunt: veluti effigies in Auleis.*
This Τὸν Θεὸν, or *Divinum ali-
quid,* is that which actuates all ;
but our Capacity not being able
to discern it, makes us fasten
either upon *Elementary Qualities,* as *Hippocrates* and *Galen*
do; or upon *Geometrical Pro-
portions,* as the Modern *Descartes*
doth. But notwithstanding we
are

are thus to feek, yet the moſt
probable Conjecture of the
Anima Mundi's Operation, is,
That *per Condenſationem & Ra-
refactionem partes Mundi Corpo-
reæ fiunt Spiritus, & ſpirituales
fiunt corpora, ſicque æternæ retro
aguntur omnia ; & cum Microcoſmus a Mundo trahit, vivit Microcoſmus: cum Mundus a Micro-
coſmo trahit, deficit Microcoſmus.*
But now to conclude my Remarques upon this

*Of Repen-
tance.*
Fourth Article, of *Re-
pentance* ; give me
leave to offer theſe few Conſi-
derations following, which may
perhaps not be impertinent for
the directing of us in this difficult Point. *Firſt,* That he that
judgeth Man, is his *Father,* and
doth look on him as a frail
Creature , obnoxious to Sin.
                              Secondly

Secondly, That he generally finds Men sin rather out of this Frail- ty, than out of any desire to of- fend his *Divine Majesty.* *Thirdly,* That if Man had been made in- wardly prone to sin, and yet destitute of all inward Means to return to him again, he had been not onely remediless in himself, but more miserable than it could be supposed an *Infinite Goodness* did at first create, and doth still perpetuate Humane kind. *Fourthly,* That *Man* can do no more on his part, for the satisfying of *Divine Justice,* than to be *heartily sorry* and *repent* him of his *Sins,* as well as to en- deavour through his Grace to return to the Right way, from which through his Transgressi- on he had erred: Or if this did not suffice for the making of

his

his Peace, that the *Supreme God,*
by inflicting some Temporal
Punishment in this Life, might
satisfie his own *Juftice.   Fifthly,
and laftly,* That if Temporal Punifhment in this Life were too
little for the Sin committed,
he might yet inflict a greater
Punifhment hereafter in the
other Life, however, without
giving *eternal Damnation* to
thofe, who (if not for the love
of Goodnefs) yet at leaft upon
fenfe of Punifhment, would not
fin eternally.   Notwithftanding, fince thefe things may
again be controverted, I fhall
infift only upon this one *univer-
fally acknowledged Propofition,*
viz. *That Repentance is the onely
known and publick Means which
on our part is required for fatif-
fying the Divine Juftice, and*
                              returning

returning to the Right way of serving God.

Of Reward and Punishment after Death.

As to the Fifth and last Article, Of a Future Reward or Punishment : Tho concerning the Place, Quantity, Quality, Manner, or Duration of Reward or Punishment after this Life, there is no universal Consent or Agreement ; yet that the *Souls* of Pious, Vertuous, and Good Men enjoy a better State after this-Life, and Vicious Wicked Men a worse, is universally acknowledged by all Religions, hardly any of the *Indians* excepted ; it being congruous to Reason, and the Notions we have of Divine Justice , that Good Men

Men (especially those who were
afflicted in this Life) should receive their *Reward* hereafter, as
well as that Wicked Men (who
were happy here) should have in
the next World condign Punishment. Which I say, because
there is no other Universal Rule,
whereby to guide our Belief
concerning God's Justice hereafter; but that his Punishment
is proportionable to the Offence;
whilst *Reward* passing all Pro-
portion is given to us, not onely according to his acceptation
of our pious Endeavours and
Actions, but also according to
the Extent and Latitude of his
Infinite Goodness and Mercy,
in Creating, Redeeming, and
Preserving us.

  Now these *Five Points* may
be matter of great Joy to all
                    Men;

Men, since hereby they may perceive, that the *Universal Providence of God* hath proceeded thus far in giving Means for *Salvation* to *all Mankind*, and therein declared himself *Communis Pater*. Neither can I imagine so much as any one *Article* more in *Common Reason*, that could make Man *better*, or *more pious*, when the aforesaid *Five Articles* were rightly explicated and observed.

Merits and Satisfaction of others.

I did perceive indeed divers Points added hereunto, which gave much ease and relaxation to Mens Minds, while they were taught to trust chiefly to the Merits and Satisfaction of others, for the obtaining of their

E   Ever-

Everlafting Happinefs; fo that
although the *Doctrine* of *Good
Works* and *Repentance* were fe-
riously inculcated into Mens
Minds, yet it may be found,
that they did not ufually fo
much fix themfelves there, as
on the aforefaid Satisfaction;
while they faid, all their *Works*
were corrupt and abominable,
and that (of themfelves) they
could not fo much as think a
good Thought; and confequent-
ly pretended to *Heaven* out of
an *Implicite Faith* and *Belief*
that this Bufinefs was done to
their Hands, rather than out of
thofe Works they feemed fo
much to difclaim: Like two
Apprentices, both of equal Parts,
and bound to the fame Mafter
and Trade; when, neverthelefs,
one of them, for want of any
                              other

other Relief, depending wholly
upon his Trade, follows it dili-
gently, and grows vaftly Rich;
whereas the other (his Fellow-
Prentice) having an Expectation
of fome Paternal Eftate of Inhe-
ritance, does fo much depend
thereon, as makes him not only
neglect his *Trade*, but fall into
thofe vicious Courfes, as makes
him out-run his Eftate before he
has it: And the contrary is
rarely feen, tho not impoffible.

Predeftination and Election.

Again, I did find in others a
Doctrine of *Predeftination* fo
taught, that Men did chiefly
truft to *God's Eternal Election* of
them before all *Worlds* : For, as
they faid, there was a certain
Mafs, from which *God* (out of

E 2   his

his *good Pleasure*) chose some, and *reprobated* others. And these Men I noted to be rather inquisitive (through the help of their *Teachers*) whether they were of the Number of the *Elect*, than studious to work out their *Salvation* by the good Degrees above related: So that, although their Teachers did indeed exhort them to a *Good Life* and *Repentance*, no less than the former, yet as Men derived not the next Causes of their *Salvation* from their own *good Endeavours* or *Actions*, so much as from the *Secret Counsels of God*; so they commonly intermitted much of their proper *Duties*, as believing either they could not fall grievously, or at least that such Remedies are provided for them, as they should

should not finally perish ; From whence one may obferve, that *Vertue* hath fuffered no fmall Detriment thereby.

Merit by Good Works.

Notwithftanding all which, I would not have Men conceive, that they could by their Good Works merit any thing of *God*, (any more than a *Subject* of *England* doth of the King, by his forbearing to commit *Felo-ny* or *Treafon*) but that I hope Men may affure themfelves, that when really they do the beft they can, it were better to truft *God's Infinite Mercy* for the acceptance of thofe *Good Works*, joyned with *Faith in* and *Love to God*, than to draw Conclufi-ons of the Certainty of their

E 3   *Sal-*

Salvation from thofe fecret and hidden *Counfels* of the *Great God,* which no *Power* of *Man* can reach unto.

Remiffion of Sins.

Moreover, I found others, who, though they did not fay they could tell who were *Predeftinated,* but, in ftead thereof, recommended *Good Works*, as the moft effectual Means on our Parts for the coming to *God,* did yet otherwife teach divers things, which, being not rightly underftood, derogated not a little from the Severity of *Vertue:* For, (as they faid) they had Power to *remit Sins;* and this *Remiffion* (again) was granted upon no very difficult Terms: Men did not fear to return to

Sin

Sin again, when they found *Pardon* so easie. Which Abuse, as also some of those above-mentioned, I conceive rather to proceed from the *proneness* of Men to *Sin,* than from the *Doctrine* of their *Priests* and *Teachers.* I could enlarge my self much upon this *Argument,* but that I am unwilling to transgress my Bounds, especially since I believe my self sufficiently understood. Besides, I find I cannot speak more of these several *Doctrines,* without entring into *Controversies,* and making use of those *Polemical Weapons,* and engaging into such a *Spiritual Warfare,* which as a *Laick* I mean never to trouble my self with. However, I hope I may so far express my self, as to wish all those *Points* that concern

E 4 *Pardon*

Pardon and *Forgiveness of Sins*, in any extraordinary way, (on what Side foever) may be warily taught, and on fuch Terms, that upon what *Promife* or *Comfortable Doctrine* foever prefented to Mankind, nothing may be detracted from that *Vertue* and *Goodnefs* which ought to be the perpetual *Exercife* of our *Life*; left occafion be given to make Men more ready and bold to *fin* again: fince while Men attend chiefly to thofe *outward Helps* or *Remedies*, they ufually comply not fo' entirely with their proper *Duties*.

Now thefe *Five Articles* being thus declared, which, if Men did embrace, would alone affert a *Catholique Church*; and it being likewife demonftrated how Neceffary it is for every

Man

Man to begin there, before he descend to the whole *Context* or *Bulk* of any one *Religion*, which he may find controverted in divers *Ages* and *Countries* ; I shall now deliver the Reasons for which I principally embraced them.

First, Because there is no other open and manifest Way extant to Mankind, whereby it is possible to establish *God's Universal Providence*, which yet is his *highest Attribute*.

Secondly, That I find nothing can be added to them, which will make a Man really more *vertuous* and *good*, than the aforesaid *Five Articles* or *Points*, when they are sufficiently inculcated in Mens Hearts.

Thirdly, That however the *Doctrines* added thereto were indeed

E. 5;

deed comfortable and full of
Promife to thofe who believe
them ; yet, fince I obfervcd in
general, that Men took occafion
thereby to grow more bold in
Sinning, I began to doubt whether they did not derogate from
the Severity of *Vertue* : And be-
fides, I found that thofe Points
were more controverted , than
that the Age of any one Man
could untie and diffolve the
Intricacies in them.

Fourthly , That I found all
Myfteries, Sacraments, and *Re-*
velations, tended chiefly to the
Eftablifhment of thefe *Five Ar-*
ticles, as being at leaft the Principal End for the which thofe
Rites were ordained.

Fifthly, and laftly, That I
thought the *doing* fome *good*
Deed, fpeaking fome *good Word*,
or,

or *thinking* some *good Thought*, were more neceſſary Exerciſes of my Life, than that I ſhould omit them for any Conſiderati- on whatſoever.

Having thus therefore ſetled theſe *Five Points*, as *Fundamen- tal,* and together demonſtra- ted, that we ought to give them the firſt place in our *Re- ligion*; I ſhall come to that *Supplemental* Part, called *Faith,* which Word (as I find among *Authors*) is uſed in two divers Senſes, and thus diſtinguiſhed: *Firſt,* As it is underſtood to be a firm Aſſent given to Things paſt, upon the Credit and Au- thority of others. And, *ſecond- ly,* As it is taken for a *Faculty* of the *Soul,* laying hold and fix- ing it ſelf on *God's Providence* and *Goodneſs* hereafter, if we do the beſt we can. Where

Where we muſt obſerve;
That as the *firſt Faith* hath its
next or moſt immediate Teſtimony from Man, and conſe-
quently is true or falſe, as they
who firſt affirmed it were: So
the *ſecond Faith* is by all *Churches* held neceſſary to be uſed
as the beſt means for the uni-
ting of our *Souls* with *God*, when
true Piety and a Good Life do
concur; inſomuch as I am confident this *latter kind* of *Faith*
may be found in good Men, tho
no *Tradition* of former times e-
ver come to their Knowledge:
Whereas the other *Faith*, depending chiefly on *Revelations*,
Miracles, and *Prophecies*, hath in
it many Difficulties, as I have
ſaid before, and is not only controverted among the ſtricter
Proſelytes of it, but in a manner
rejected:

rejected by those *Nations* among
whom other *Faiths* have been
taught by their *Lawgivers*; for
all *Faiths* have been shaken; but
those only which stand upon
the *Basis* of *Common* *Reason.*

 Notwithstanding all which, as
I thought, it concerned me, a-
mong those several and miracu-
lous *Traditions*, (which were
not impossible to have been true,
if *God* so pleased,) not to distrust
and doubt of all, *Wherefore* I
applyed my self chiefly to the
Christian Faith contained in the
Holy Bible, as having in it more
exact *Precepts* for the Teaching
us a *good life* and *repentance,*
than any other Book whatsoever that I could meet with: and
besides I found my self (through
Gods Providence) born in the
Christian Church, and instructed
      even;

even from my Infancy in the *Holy Doctrines* drawn from thence. But as together I observed many things taught in the said *Church,* which were not only vehemently opposed by other *Christian Churches,* but also repudiated in their chief parts among other *Nations :* So, I found no such solid *Foundation* to build this my *Faith* upon, as the *Authority* in general of the *Christian Church ;* resolving according to the saying of a Learned *Father, That those things I never had known without the Church, I never had believed without it.* Neither did the Controversies among them much move me, since being a meer *Laick,* I had neither Will nor Leisure to engage my self in the clearing of those doubts; the scruples

scruples of those variously a-
gitated disputes by Men equally Learned, being of such in-
tricacy, that I saw more and
more might be said about them,
than that I should presume to
determine any thing by the
Judgment of the best Authors
I could peruse on either side:
So that for my *final resolution,*
I thought the best *grounds* of
my *Faith* ought to be taken
from those points which were
piously assented to by all *Chri-*
stians, and might aptly consist
with my aforementioned *Five*
Articles ; But for the *disputes*
and *controversies* of Learned
Men, to lay them aside, until
they were agreed amongst
themselves ; and in the mean
while to attend a *good life,* and ;
repentance, assuring my self, that

in

in the quality of a *Laick* or *Secular Person*, my time was better imployed so, than in the inexplicable *subtleties* of the *Schoolmen*. To conclude, I embraced the *five Catholick Articles* for the Reasons above mentioned; from whence coming to the *Doctrines* of *Faith*, I believed piously, upon the *reverend Authority* of the *Church*, that which was unanimously taught by them, without any contradictions: All which I have here set down with no intention to scandalize any, but only to give a Reason as well of those *Points* which may be known, as of those which are already believed in the *Christian-Religion*: And also to induce men by these *Principles* to the *Practice* of a good life, and blessed concord among them.

themſelves; ſince having joint-
ly received theſe *five Catholick
Points*, there will be leſs occaſion of hate and diſſention about
the reſt: So that the *different
Opinions* amongſt them might
be argued with leſs *violence* and
paſſion, the *Points* wherein they
are agreed being greater *bonds*
of *Love* and *Amity* among them,
than that they ſhould be diſſolv-
ed on any leſſer occaſion. And
certainly, unleſs the *Method* I
have here propoſed be effectual
to this purpoſe, I ſee no hope
that any good Reconciliation
can follow among the *Principal
Sects* of the *Chriſtian Religion*;
ſince the one *affirming* the *Scri-
pture* to be the *ſole Judge* of
Controverſies, and the other ſay-
ing that the *Church* alone ſhould
determine them, they ſeem like
perſons

perſons in variance, who diſa-
greeing about their *Arbitrators*
or *Judges*, are hopeleſs that the
buſineſs in Queſtion between
them ſhould ever come to a *juſt*
Tryal, and find an indifferent or
equal Deciſion. Now upon all
that hath been ſaid, give me
leave to raiſe theſe few *Queries*,
and ſo conclude.

*Queries proving the validity of
the five Articles.*

1. *Whether* there be any *True
God*, but he that uſeth *Univerſal
Providence* concerning the *means*
of coming to him?

2. *Whether* theſe *means* appear univerſally otherwiſe, than
in our aforeſaid *five Catholick
Articles* ?

3. *Whether* any thing can be
added

added to thefe *Five Principles,*
that may tend to make a Man
more *honeft, vertuous,* or a *better
Man ?*

4. *Whether* any things that
are added to thefe *Five Principles* from the *Doctrine* of *Faith,*
be not *uncertain* in their *Original ?*

5. Suppofing the *Originals*
true, *Whether* yet they be not
uncertain in their *Explications,*
fo that unlefs a Man read all
Authors, fpeak with all *Learned
Men,* and know all *Languages,*
it be not impoffible to come to
a clear *Solution* of *all Doubts?*

6. Suppofing all *true* in their
Originals, and in their *Explications, Whether* yet they be fo
good for the inftructing of Mankind, that bring *Pardon* of *Sin*
upon fuch eafie Terms, as to believe

lieve the Bufinefs is done to our Hands ? And,

. 7. *Whether* this *Doctrine* doth not derogate from *Vertue* and *Goodnefs*, whilft our beft Actions are reprefented as Imperfect and Sinful, and that it is impoffible to keep the *Ten Commandments*, fo as *God* will accept our *Actions*, doing the beft we can?

8. *Whether* fpeaking *good Words*, thinking *good Thoughts*, and doing *good Actions*, be not the juft Exercife of a Mans Life? Or that without embracing of the forefaid *Five Principles* or *Fundamentals* , it be poffible to keep *Peace* among Men, that *God* may be well ferved ?

9. *Whether* the forefaid *Five Principles* do not beft agree with the *Precepts* given in the *Ten Commandments*, and with the *Two Precepts*

Precepts of *Jesus Christ,* viz. *To love God above all, and our Neighbour as our selves?* As well as with the Words of *St. Peter, That in every Nation he which feareth God, and worketh Righteousness, is accepted of God?*

10. *Whether* the *Doctrine* of *Faith* can by *Humane Reason* be supposed or granted to be *Infallible,* unless we are infallibly assured, that those who teach this *Doctrine* do know the *Secret Counsels* of God?

11. *Whether* all things in the *Scriptures,* (besides the *Moral Part,* which agrees with our *Five Principles*) such as *Prophecy, Miracles,* and *Revelations* depending on the *History,* may not be so far examined, as to be made appear by what *Authority* they are or may be received?

12. *Whether*

12. *Whether* in *Humane Reason* any one may or ought to be convinced by *one single Testimony*, so far as to believe things contrary to, or besides *Reason*?

13. *And lastly, Whether,* if it were granted they had *Revelations,* I am obliged to accept of anothers *Revelation* for the *Ground* of my *Faith* ? Especially if it doth any ways oppose these *Five Articles,* that are grounded

The Law of Nature unalterable.

upon the *Law* of Nature, which is *God's* universal *Magna Charta,* Enacted by the *All-wise* and *Supreme Being* from the *beginning* of the *World,* and therefore not to be destroyed or altered by every *whiffling Proclamation* of an *Enthusiast.*

Finally, Submitting this Discourse to any Impartial and Judicious licious *Reader*, I shall conclude with the *Saying* of *Justin Martyr*, p. 83. Καὶ οἱ μετὰ λόγυ, &c. *That all those who lived according to the Rule of Reason, were Christians, notwithstanding that they might have been accounted as Atheists :* such as, among the Greeks, *were* Socrates, Heraclius, *and the like ; and among the* Barbarians, Abraham *and* Azarias : *For all those who lived, or do now live, according to the Rule of Reason, are Christians, and in an assured quiet condition.* Apol. cont. Tryph.

F I N I S.

DO NOT REMOVE
OR
MUTILATE CARD

Check Out More Titles From HardPress Classics Series In this collection we are offering thousands of classic and hard to find books. This series spans a vast array of subjects – so you are bound to find something of interest to enjoy reading and learning about.

Subjects:
Architecture
Art
Biography & Autobiography
Body, Mind &Spirit
Children & Young Adult
Dramas
Education
Fiction
History
Language Arts & Disciplines
Law
Literary Collections
Music
Poetry
Psychology
Science
…and many more.

Visit us at www.hardpress.net

CPSIA information can be obtained
at www.ICGtesting.com
Printed in the USA
BVHW071003150819
555975BV00018B/1722/P